Testi

This book is a poetic gift to oneself. The clear, practical writing compels the soul to start the journey with the self. After digesting this book, you will be moved to pay attention to your life!

~Gwen Ritch, Yoga Instructor

These beautiful, simple practices are powerful and profound, and all that's required to benefit from them is a few minutes at a time and a willingness to engage. A very useful and forgiving companion for one's personal path.

~Lorae Marsten, Yoga teacher, Healer, Vedic Astrologer
www.LoraeMarsten.com

You'll find this book to be full of wonder and magic. It refocused me and helped me to remember what I believe in, how I want to live my life daily, and how, by shifting my perspective, I become a better version of myself.

~Tracy Moen
www.fullaenergy.com

The simple instructions in this book bring one's life under the microscope. In being mindful, you will learn how to be compassionate with yourself, and then with others. A compassionate mind is a boundless mind. Make yourself a cup of tea, and sit down with this book right now!

~Judith Hirst, ATP® CBP®
www.AngelsAndAncestors.com

Through a series of concepts and affirmations, "Living the Mindful Way" invites the reader to contemplate and practice ideals that are the keystones of a fulfilled life. From conscious breathing, to self-forgiveness, to minding your thoughts and much more, this book provides us with a companion to support us on what can sometimes be a tumultuous life journey.

~ Timothy Sebastian, Retired Educator,
Entrepreneur, Philanthropist

You have in your hands a treasure. Inside are methods to create new mental habits of self-awareness and self-mastery! 5 minutes a day will create new paradigms for your life. I started today with these practices.

~ Beth Haley, Life Coach
www.BethHaley.com

LIVING THE MINDFUL WAY

85 Everyday Mindfulness Practices for Finding Inner Peace

Sharon L Horstead

www.LivingTheMindfulWay.com

Living The Mindful Way: 85 Everyday Mindfulness Practices For Finding Inner Peace

ISBN: 0986777501
EAN-13: 9780986777509

Dedicated to
My Higher Self

Thank you, Wise One.
I'm listening!

Dear Catherine,

Let yourself blossom like
the beautiful flower you are.
Blessings,
Sharon

One spinning atom
makes a small shift to the left.
A new world is born.

~SLH

Be YOU, Be Love, Be Peace

Acknowledgments

Where do I begin to give thanks for all the blessings in my life and the help I've received with this book? There are so many who have contributed not only to this project but to me becoming Who I Am.

I love and thank my parents, Janet and Frank, for inviting me to this world, for keeping me safe, and encouraging me to be and do my best.

I am grateful to so many friends, particularly Jaci, Gwen, Judy, Beth, Tim, Tracy, and Lorae, for giving feedback and keeping me grounded and moving forward with this book. There are many others who have loved me, and shared life with me, and have always mirrored back to me the best of myself.

I am grateful to many spiritual teachers, some of whom I've only met in books and others I've had the privilege of being guided by personally. Thank you to Leonard Orr, Chuck and Lency Spezzano, Louise Hay, Wayne Dyer, Jack Kornfield, Thich Nhat Hanh, and His Holiness, the Dalai Lama.

And a special thank you to Gary Vurnum for the great care he has taken with helping me to put this book into print and send it out to the world. He is a real blessing on my journey of service to others. Check out Gary's awesome books at www.92Tips.com.

Introduction

Life was never meant to be a daily struggle. I'm sure that you picked up this book because there is a part of you that knows that. You're looking for a way to experience more ease, peace, and happiness. And you think that meditation might be a way to find that. Well, it can be. The problem for most of us who want to meditate, including me, is that we think it's going to be hard, or it will take hours a day, or it will turn us into some blissed out hippie who can never get anything done. None of that has to be the truth, unless that becomes your choice.

Even though I know better, I had started to believe the lies my mind was telling me. I was getting very stressed. Parts of my life were unraveling because I was chasing neurotic goals that brought me no joy.

I wanted to meditate and looked at the different disciplines and methods. I didn't want to sabotage myself before I even began, so I chose mindfulness. I didn't even have to become a Buddhist to benefit from this practice of paying attention and looking deep inside my heart instead of listening to the chatter in my head.

I started with simple processes, five minutes at a time. The more I listened to myself, the easier life became and the happier and more peaceful I became. Life still gets messy, that's the human journey of a lifetime, but I developed a healthy way to respond to life, to engage with it, and even thrive because I have found my truth. I gained a deep understanding of Who I Am, what my life is about, and what Life itself is about. My level of self-confidence is becoming unshakable. I am beginning to see what I am capable of and I have realized that there are even greater things inside me yet to be revealed. It's exciting.

All this talk of looking inside yourself might make you a bit anxious. Many people are afraid they will confirm that they really are not good enough. Or that they really are powerful but accepting that power will require too much of them. Each of these fears is a lie. When you have the courage to seek, the Truth will set you free. The moment you first understand with all of your being the magnificence of who you are your life will change forever. The world and your life will become a joy and you will have a measure of peace that you have not known before.

Mindfulness is no small thing. It doesn't have to be a deeply spiritual pursuit, but it is profound. Great rewards come from being able to simply relax and find peace. If you think it will be hard, scary, or time-consuming, you may never start. I wrote this book to help launch your journey in an easy manner. When I was ready to begin, I had to wade through a whole lot of poetic writing and cryptic stories to get to the meat of the matter. But reading another's flowery words about mindfulness will not bring you much benefit. The map is not the territory. The only way to know its value is to do it for yourself.

That is why each of these 85 practices is short on description. Read one a day. When you contemplate and actually do it, it should not take you much more than five minutes. You may find that some of the practices seem to contradict each other. Get curious about why that might be and what benefits are to be gained. Actually, get curious about everything in your life. That's the essence of mindfulness. Notice what's going on inside and around you and how it all affects your experience of life.

You may notice that I did not include a practice about Love. Love is our natural state of being. As you work with these practices, connecting with your heart and removing doubt, fear, and limitations, you will find love is your inner core—love for yourself, your family and friends, your business, the world, and all of Life. Express that love and you will find your inner peace.

Your journey with the practices in this book will be different than mine, but it will be no less transformative. When you gain a bit of momentum, massive change happens quickly. Your inner wisdom, once you have begun, will reveal to you additional ways of furthering your growth.

Radical transformation doesn't have to be radically hard. You can do anything for five minutes. You are worth spending that short amount of time to find out who you are, what you really want, and what you are really capable of. Sometimes, one five minute session might bring an epiphany and clarity that completely changes your life. At other times, what began as five minutes might stretch as long as an hour and bring you to deep knowing. Then again, five minutes consistently over a number of days can lead you to a meaningful realization. One day you will turn around and find that you are living fully in the present moment and have created the peaceful, happy life you always wanted.

I wish for you awareness of your magnificence, courage to explore your deep places, strength to live your truth, and many present moments of boundless peace and joy.

Blessings,

Sharon

Be YOU, Be Love, Be Peace

*"Your hearts know in silence
the secrets of the days and nights."*

~ Kahlil Gibran

Contents

Breathing in, I calm my body. Breathing out, I smile.

 1

BREATHE

Taking hold of your breath is mindfulness itself. Whenever you find yourself distracted, concentrating on your breath will return you to the present moment and to communion with your whole being. To be able to do so is a miracle.*

Pay attention to your breath. As you breathe in, know that you are breathing in. As you breathe out, know that you are breathing out. Focus on allowing your body to relax into calmness. Allow a soft, warm smile to light your face. Allow your breath to reunite your body, mind, and heart.

* Breathwork is so beneficial that I recommend you find a good book or teacher to help you explore.

I am focused and engaged in every moment of my life.

2

ENGAGE

Multi-tasking fragments your being, causing stress and draining your energy. Mindfulness unifies your being and increases your energy. Being present in everything you do creates peace because you will be whole. Focus your attention fully when you are brushing your teeth, spending time with others, or doing your taxes. This is *living* each moment and the way to peace and happiness.

I dance to the beat of a
different drummer.
I groove to my natural rhythm.

 3

RHYTHM

We are all calibrated to a different frequency. You may be high strung and active all the time (in a healthy way). You may be geared to bursts of massive energy followed by periods of deep rest. You may operate at a steady pace or move a bit slow. Be still for five minutes and feel your natural rhythm and vibe.

The more often you operate at your natural tempo, the more peaceful you will feel inside and the easier your life will flow.

I sparkle and shine.
My light transforms
every situation.

4

SPARKLE

When children are afraid of the dark, turning on a light instantly removes the terror. You are a jewel of light. Your consciousness sparkles like a diamond and can shift any dark situation.

Only practicing mindfulness will dispel the illusion of darkness and free you from fear. Look inside and find your light. You are a powerful and unlimited being. Nothing can truly hurt you. Sparkle wherever you go.

I love and appreciate my body.
It is the temple of my soul.

 5

BODY

Mindfulness is not escaping the body or devaluing it. How would you live this glorious life without your body? Rejoice in your physical being. It is truly the home in which YOU reside.

BE fully in your body. Spend five minutes showering your body with love and gratitude for how it supports you and gives you the means to do, have, and be what you want. For it is in this physical existence that your spirit expands.

I inhale deeply, exhale fully.
I am energized
and full of Life.

6

ENERGIZE

Breathing deeply fills your body with precious oxygen and literally infuses you with life force energy.

Breathe consciously. Inhale slowly through your nostrils, filling your lungs. Picture golden white light coming in through your nose and spreading through your body, healing and renewing as it goes. As soon as your lungs fill, exhale through your nose, releasing tension and negativity. Begin again to inhale as soon as your lungs are empty. It only takes a few breaths to feel fully charged.

I was born with a
Powerful Purpose.
I share my gifts every day.

 7

PURPOSE

Living your purpose cannot be done from your head. It involves your soul-level gifts and is, in the most profound way, Who You Are. Purpose goes beyond having a mission, which may be only one way of expressing your contribution to Life.

Be still and listen. Your heart will remind you what your gifts are and why you are here. You will discover that you have power others don't have or won't use because they are afraid. Show them the way and give yourself to every moment of your life.

I set aside time
to look at my life.
I'm worth it.

8

LOOK

Responding to what arises as it happens is the essence of mindfulness. It is also helpful to deliberately look inside. Set a timer that has a gentle alarm and sit still for five minutes. Give yourself permission to just BE. Observe the thoughts that enter your head and just allow them to float by. Idle chatter might be all you notice. Or something of great importance might finally have the space to reveal itself.

At times it will feel right to reset your timer. By starting small and not forcing, you will naturally develop a meditation practice.

My body is wise.
It tells me what I need to know.
I'm listening.

 9

LISTEN

Scientists have learned that each and every cell in your body communicates with each and every other cell. Hectic living removes your conscious mind from this vast network of communication and it is easy to miss warnings that your body sends you.

Close your eyes and be still. Starting at the top of your head, ask your body what you need to know for your wellbeing. Scan all the way down to your toes. Listen for answers as you go along. You might hear some surprising news. Thank your body and act on its wise advice.

I can only choose which
thoughts to focus on,
not every thought I have.

10 🪷

THOUGHTS

You cannot consciously choose your every thought. Mostly, they just are. They may surface from your subconscious mind and have no connection to present reality. They may just be floating in the collective consciousness waiting for someone to notice them. Or they may bubble up from your heart and reveal your true nature. Once a thought has arisen, then you can consciously decide what to do with it. Listen to your thoughts for five minutes. Then choose which ones you will give your attention to and which ones you will release.

Love, fear, and neutrality
are normal, human emotions.
I allow them to energize my life.

 11

FEELINGS

Feelings and emotions are the barometer of your internal environment. They are the electric current that naturally illuminates your awareness like flashes of lightning.

An initial thought sparks your primary feelings of love, fear, and neutrality. Each gives rise to the other secondary emotions, mental states, and physical sensations that you experience. Every time you pinch off your feelings, you dampen your field of vital energy.

In this moment, be alert and become aware of the feeling of love, fear, or neutrality lying underneath whatever you are observing.

I breathe in the Mountain.
I breathe out Silence.
I am rock solid.

12

STABILITY

At times, your emotions may make you feel vulnerable and overwhelm you. When you become the mountain, you are more powerful and steady than your emotions. Sit in a stable position. Breathing in, see yourself as a mountain. Breathing out, know that you are solid. When you are silent and mindful, you connect to your immovable core.

I am powerful
in the NOW.

 13

PRESENT

Your memories of the past and your dreams and worries for the future are experienced in the present moment. And your perceptions of each cause chaos or peace and affect your mind, body, and spirit right now.

Allow the past to inform you and the future to inspire you, but you can only make your choices and live NOW. Bring your attention to this moment and be here, NOW. Respond to what is NOW.

I grow beyond my childhood hurts. I acknowledge, then lovingly release my past.

14

PAST

The vast majority of your subconscious mind was programmed when you were an innocent child. Before your logical mind developed, you experienced your world on a purely emotionajl level. What you now think should have been insignificant, may have turned you upside down then.

When a negative thought or memory bubbles up from your subconscious, logic alone will not dissolve it. Be compassionate with yourself. Acknowledge the pain you felt that created that thought or belief. You no longer need to hold this misunderstanding. Breathe love into this new awareness, let go, and return to your original innocence.

I open the door to my future
and joyfully walk
toward the horizon.

 15

FUTURE

Be still, breathe deeply and calmly. Imagine walking to a door. Open it and look onto a beautiful landscape. Look beyond what you see with your mind. It can only project based on the past. See with your heart which knows the future. Where does it want to lead you? Feel the forward pull and follow it. If you feel a snag of resistance, allow the gentle winds of change to caress you and blow away whatever holds you back. *Don't linger*. Come back and *live it* with joy and gratitude!

I am open to change.
It is always an
exciting opportunity to grow.

16 🪷

CHANGE

The only constant in life is change. Everything evolves and grows or breaks down and dies. Resisting change only causes suffering. When you are willing to embrace change and see it as an adventure, then you will *live*.

What are you resisting? How does it feel? How would life be different if you took a chance?

In the darkest storm,
my inner beacon
shines the way to safety.

 17

BEACON

Sailors have relied for centuries on lighthouses and beacons to find safe passage on the seas. You have an inner light that shines for you, giving warnings and pointing the safe route.

When your seas are rough, be still and see the light shining in you. As the beam shines around, notice what comes to light that you didn't see before. Are there rocks up ahead to avoid? Is there a deep channel that will lead you to a protected harbor? With light all around you, where are you being guided?

Everything I need to succeed
is already inside me.
I am enough.

18

ENOUGH

How many times have you talked yourself out
of an inspired idea because you thought it was
too big for you to do? Did you let it pass by
because you didn't feel strong enough, or
smart enough, or brave enough?

You have your own unique brilliance, skills,
talents, perspective, and creativity. It's all
there inside you. You are only powerless when
you allow your self-talk to defeat you. What
inspired idea will you talk yourself *into*?

When I take the first step,
I celebrate.
I enjoy the journey.

 19

STEPS

How many times have you heard, "The journey of 1,000 miles begins with a single step?" It is so easy to forget to live by this ancient wisdom.

Do something today, anything, to step in the direction of whatever it is your heart wants to do, have, or be. Anytime you move forward instead of staying stuck is a joyous occasion. Give yourself a hand, do a little dance, then take another step. Find as many reasons as you can to celebrate.

I let the sun shine in.
I bask in the glory of Who I Am.

20 🪷

WORTH

Next time someone lavishes you with praise, don't shrug it off. Soak it up and say, "You're right. Thank you." When someone gives you a gift, be grateful and know that you deserve it. When someone offers you help, receive it. Allow all the love and all the good into your life. Stay humble and don't let it go to your head, but being mindful means accepting your honest and true worth.

It's okay to say NO.
I set boundaries
and protect what *I* want.

 21

BOUNDARIES

Over-commitment has almost become a disease. Assess what you say yes to. Is it what someone else wants or what social conditioning trained you to believe you "should" do?

If it is something you can do or give with joy, go right ahead. If it feels heavy or takes you too far away from what you need to be happy, then gracefully decline. What feels true?

I pamper myself regularly.
It is critical for my wellbeing
and peace of mind.

22

SELF-CARE

Rest and rejuvenation is not a luxury. Self-care is vital if you are going to be happy, creative, and productive. Long baths, walks in nature, time with family and friends, healthy food, or a tropical holiday may be what you really need to be balanced, strong, and vibrant. Schedule "me time" now.

Walking in nature is medicine.
I connect to the earth
and find my peaceful center.

 23

NATURE

There are many energies in nature that are healing. Fresh air filling your lungs detoxifies. Ozone from ocean spray or lightning storms vitalizes. Treading on the earth grounds you.

Observing the stars fixes your place in the cosmos. Observing plants and animals fixes your place in the world. Sights, sounds, smells, tastes, textures, and emotions fix your place in your body.

Spend a few minutes, or a few days, outdoors. Allow nature to heal all aspects of your being and return you back to center.

I bless my food.
Giving thanks enriches it.

24

NOURISHMENT

Everything is energy, so the quality of energy that you put into your body is important. Every bite of food you put into your mouth will either nourish you or poison you.

Sending love and gratitude to all those involved in bringing your food to your table and to all life forms who gave themselves for your nourishment will raise the vibration of the food. Being mindful of every bite will make your food taste better, be healthier, and satisfy you fully.

I allow a flickering flame
to soothe my mind.
Fire is good for my soul.

 25

FIRE

Since man discovered how to control fire, we have used its magical power for meditation and healing. A dancing flame invokes deep focus. Sit by an open fire or in front of a candle flame at eye level. Your mind will shut out other stimuli and calm down.

Fire will also burn negativity from your energy field or aura. This cleansing effect compounds the meditative effect of fire for an overall feeling of wellbeing. Bring fire back into your daily life and let it transform you.*

* Do not play with fire. Respect it and always take appropriate safety precautions.

I make time to smell the roses.
Their beauty elevates
my mood and my whole being.

26

ROSES

Roses have a very pure, high, and loving vibration. It's no wonder men love to give them and women love to receive them.

The next time you walk past a garden full of roses, lean over the fence and inhale the sweet fragrance. Walk down the grocery store floral aisle and have a good sniff. It's free and doesn't hurt the roses. Fill yourself with the essence of Love.

I have incredible beauty inside waiting to burst into blossom.

 27

BLOSSOM

Do you know your true beauty? Do you know your full potential?

Imagine yourself as a tightly-folded flower bud, starting small and green. The vibrant color, the intoxicating fragrance, the delicate petals are there, waiting to explode and express their glory in the world at precisely the right moment of ripeness.

There is much inside you, ripening, getting ready to unfurl. You are an exquisite gift to all of Creation. And Creation's gift to you is that you can blossom again and again.

When I look in the mirror,
I see past the freckles and wrinkles and say, "I Love YOU."

28

SELF-LOVE

Do you ever look in the mirror to just sincerely appreciate yourself? This might be the hardest thing you ever do.

You are a magnificent creation, an innocent and lovable being. Look in the mirror without self-criticism. Say your name, and say, "I love you," until you can feel genuine esteem for who you are. If this is hard for you, turn out the lights and bring a candle to your mirror. Just as a lover is more radiant by candlelight, so will you be. It will be easier to see your beauty in this positive glow.

I sing my song with glee.
I make a joyful noise!

 29

EXPRESSION

We all have music, or poetry, or paintings, or stories inside of us that are aching to get out. Set them free and feel the deep satisfaction of expressing yourself. Who cares if you sing out of tune? Do it just for you. Then decide if it feels right to share it with someone else.

I move closer to others
and closer to my Self
every time I drop judgment.

30 ❀

NON-JUDGMENT

Do you judge others by how they look, or what they say or do? When you do that, you create a barrier between you and Life.

Every person is a unique, beautiful expression of Life. If you find yourself judging, step back for a moment. See if you can distinguish the difference between the behavior and the person. When you can do that, you will see their divinity. In that vision lies the discovery of your own divinity.

I express gratitude for at least
two ordinary things every day.

 31

GRATITUDE

Be grateful for the mailman, the sun shining
through your window, or your coffee cup.

It is easy to give thanks for life's miracles.
Notice what you take for granted. Be thankful
that parts of your life are so effortless.

Life's a beach.
I let my breath roll like
ocean waves and get in the *flow*.

32

FLOW

Life is a constant flow of giving and receiving. Fear, doubt, busyness, or holding on turn it into a stagnant pool.

When you are feeling particularly tense, stop for a moment and picture yourself lying on a warm, sandy beach. Harmonize your breathing with the steady flow of the waves. As you breathe out, a wave lands on shore. As you breathe in, the wave returns to the sea. You don't have to breathe particularly deeply, just rhythmically. This is how newborn babies breathe. Notice how you feel more prepared to roll with whatever is happening around you.

I remove all outside influences
and enjoy the peace within.

 33

GAPS

It can be difficult to empty your mind. It will chatter on and give a running commentary on everything in your life. If you constantly feed this Monkey Mind and let it run wild, it will create chaos and you will go bananas. To experience inner peace, remove external stimuli and distractions like television, food, and negative people for a short time. You will begin to be aware of gaps of silence between your thoughts. Rejoice!

Life is a grand Mystery.
I dance with the Unknowable.

34 🪷

MYSTERY

Life is a big mess of paradox, conundrum, and hidden truth. This is the human condition and you might as well accept it. Creativity is what makes us divine but it cannot flow when we stay safe in routine or need to plan for every contingency before we make a move. Be comfortable with not knowing all the answers. Relax, take a step; the next one will be revealed. Enjoy the dance.

Stress is an inside job.
So is peace.
I choose peace.

🪷 35

INTERPRETATION

What happens in your life isn't as important as how you interpret and internalize. Events are neutral; your mind gives them meaning.

Focus on something you judge as good and see if you can find what would not be good about it. Focus on something you judge as not good and see if you can find what would be good about it. Notice the fluctuations of stress and peace inside you depending on how you interpret the situation. That is the power that awareness gives you.

I greet everyone with a smile.
Love and joy flow from me
and I feel *GOOD*.

36

SMILE

There is a phenomenon called the Duchenne
Smile. When your smile causes crinkles around
your eyes, your body changes. It relaxes and
feels good because the action stimulates your
left cerebral cortex. For that moment, you
cannot be sad, or tense, or in pain. Your heart
will soften and open a bit. Practice smiling
fully at everyone you meet. It doesn't matter
if they smile back. Do it to feel peace and joy
in your body. If someone does smile back,
bonus!

I choose to be happy.
I let my heart be light
in this moment.

 37

HAPPINESS

Keeping up with the Joneses will make you crazy. Your happiness is not dependent on material things or conditions. Nor can it be pursued as a means to escape suffering. It is a state of mind arising from a wise and gracious heart.

Spend five minutes of quiet time. Close your eyes and see yourself weighed down by all your defenses of fear, depression, confusion, and aggression. Deliberately peel each layer off of you until you reveal your innate goodness. Happiness is that feeling of light-heartedness. It will not remain, but you can always choose happiness again. Throw some love into your meditation and you have a recipe for JOY.

I do unto myself
as I would have
others do unto me.

38

GOLD

This is a twist on the Golden Rule. Do you treat others better than you treat yourself? Do others treat you better than you treat yourself? It is important to know that you, like anyone, deserve to be treated like gold.

Speak kindly to yourself. Drop your judgment. Praise and encourage yourself. Be your own best friend. The Creator that is wise enough to manifest universes was wise enough to put you here. Why would anyone be more important than you?

Breathing in, I am still water.
Breathing out, I see things
as they are.

 39

REFLECTING

Like the moon reflecting on still water, the Divine wishes to reflect Itself through you. How can that happen if you are agitated and troubled? Be still and picture a smooth, calm lake. Looking into the water, you can see yourself and all of Life without distortion, illuminated by the pure light of the Cosmos.

I live by my own rules.
My heart knows what is
right, good, and true.

40

MORALITY

Strict and rigid rules, dogma, and ideologies are nothing more than someone else's attempt to relieve their own fears, control others, and meet their own needs. Blindly adhering to societal conditioning detaches you from your own awareness of what is ethical, virtuous, and honest. Stop playing someone else's game. Access your divinity and all your actions will naturally be beautiful and right.

I drop the blame game and
take full responsibility for my life.
I am FREE.

 41

RESPONSIBILITY

It sounds funny that taking responsibility will bring freedom. The truth is that when you blame anyone or anything for circumstances in your life, you are giving away your power. It is the thoughts *you* think, the emotions *you* feel, and the actions *you* take that create your life. That is awesome power and with it you can manifest anything you want. Will you claim your power and set yourself free?

I recognize what is within my
control and what is not.
I do what I can.

42

CONTROL

Be mindful of what is outside of your control
and do not allow those things to weigh you
down. For example, the state of the world
economy is not in your control but the state of
your own economy is. Do what you can to
keep your finances organized, get out of debt,
and be mindful of opportunities to increase
your income.

The larger problems of society may take some
time to correct. Make a difference in your
own life and the lives of those you love. As
your personal situation begins to improve, you
can join with others to tackle the world.

I weigh my options.
When I am mindful, decisions
and choices become clear.

🪷 43

WEIGHING

When you have to make a decision or choice, connect first with your heart. Close your eyes and hold your hands in front of you. Mentally place each aspect of what needs to be decided into your hands. Weigh each one and determine which is heavier. Based on what the decision is, the heavier one might feel more substantial and meaty, or it might feel more burdensome and tiring. Trust your inner knowing.

Something is only a mistake
if I don't learn from it.
I make smart changes.

44

RESULTS

When you're busy living your life, trying new things, you are bound to experience some challenges. Rather than judging something as a mistake, call it "unintended results." This is not a whitewash but a perspective that allows you to respond mindfully rather than fight, flee, or freeze.

Be still, tune in, assess the results without judgment or reproach, make adjustments, then take inspired action. Any single course correction or a combination of several will get you back in the flow.

I easily return
to the present moment,
prompted by little cues.

🪷 45

CUES

Just like Pavlov's dogs, your mind can be trained to react to certain triggers. Set the intention to come back to the present when something like the phone ringing occurs. Choose something that happens regularly in your day. You could also set an alarm on your watch to prompt you. As time goes by, you will rely less on these constant reminders and it will be easier to be mindful regularly.

I begin my day Happy.
My intention sets the tone
for me to follow.

46 ⚜

WAKING

When you first wake up, notice what you are thinking, what your emotions are, and how your body feels. If you're not excited by what you observe, choose how you want to feel. Breathe into that feeling until it vibrates through your whole being.

One of the gifts of mindfulness is that as your life slowly begins to change you wake up already happy.

I pay attention to the red flags
waving in my life.
I deal with them boldly and quickly.

 47

COURAGE

Ignoring urgent matters because they make
you anxious will only cause more suffering if
you delay. Stress and other consequences will
pile up. Ask yourself what is at the root of
your procrastination and address it. Have the
courage to deal with uncomfortable things
before they become truly painful. Then savor
the sigh of relief that rushes over you.

I give myself time
to really enjoy my life.
I seek balance.

48 🪷

BALANCE

It's tempting to think that if you just go faster and cram more things into your life, you'll have more fun and happiness. Don't buy it.

Rushing through things may get them done, but you'll miss some of the juiciest nuances of life. Find a balance that allows you time to experience the richness of the moment without getting stuck in it.

I am open to endless possibilities.
I am in the flow and see
there is always a Plan B.

🪷 49

POSSIBILITIES

Life is full of surprises and things may not always go according to plan. When stress hormones are running through your body, you will fight, flee, or freeze. Breathe slowly and deeply until you flow. Then you will see how creative you are. You will never be stuck. You are an unlimited being with unlimited options. Which of the many will you choose?

Breathing in, I create space.
Breathing out, I am free.

50

SPACE

To be happy, there must be space around you and also inside you. You need room to breathe and to move. Too many worries and pressures tie you up. Plans and expectations bind and imprison you. Breathe in and imagine yourself in the middle of the Cosmos. Breathe out and imagine yourself free of attachments. Give yourself space to BE.

I am at peace with the amount
of stuff I have around me.
I am comfortable.

 51

FULLNESS

An empty mind, and life, doesn't always mean a happy one. Each person has their own level of sufficiency. Be present to your environment —is it too crammed full or is it too sterile? Do you have what you need to feel creative? Is there too much for you to be calm? Be honest with yourself about what you genuinely need for comfort and peace.

I am mindful of
the perfectionism trap.
I do the best I can and am happy.

52

PERFECTION

The need to be perfect may hide a fear that was programmed when you were a child. When you find yourself getting bogged down or stressed out, breathe. Ask yourself what is at the root of the situation and what you can do to shift it. What can you let go of so you can move forward with grace, ease, and speed without sacrificing quality? Sometimes good enough is good enough.

Every day matters.
I listen to my heart's dreams
and joyfully follow its lead.

 53

ACTION

Mindfulness is not living in your head. Endless dreaming can create misery. Doing can create peace. When you are aware of your heart's desires, not acting on them leads to frustration and sadness. You will regret most the dreams you let die. What dream needs your attention today? Act.

I allow my Monkey Mind
to reveal my obstacles.
Then I align with the Truth.

54 🪷

ALIGNMENT

The Law of Attraction will always fail to deliver satisfactory results if you set neurotic intentions generated by your mind. Even if they come from your heart, your subconscious mind must be aligned with your intentions.

Write an affirmation for something you want. For instance, "I am richly abundant and financially free." Just sit and allow all the negative chatter that comes up. Great! That is what stands in your way. A few moments of mindfulness will show you the truth. Breathe that in deeply, then step aside and let Spirit do its thing.

The picture of my life is panoramic.
I relax, even though I can't
see it all in this moment.

 55

DIRECTION

Your Higher Self is all-seeing, all-knowing, and all-powerful. It has the map to where your life is headed and will never lead you astray. Synchronicities are like markers on the trail. Sometimes you need to let go of the reins and trust that you're being guided in the right direction.

My mind is my friend.
I give it good thoughts
to work with.

56 🪷

DATA

Some will tell you that your mind is not your friend, that it will try to sabotage you. This is not true. The subconscious mind has no will of its own. Like software on your computer, what comes out depends on the data you put in.

When your mind tells you things like you are not safe, or you will make a fool of yourself, or you will fail, it does so because that is the data that went in. Give your mind new data and it will give you a different result. Then it will feel like your friend.

I listen to my intuition.
It knows things
my conscious mind doesn't.

 57

INTUITION

Have you ever had a gut feeling that you ignored, and later wished you hadn't? When you are mindful, you connect easily with your intuition—that part of you that has access to a higher and broader field of information than is available to your conscious mind.

What is your intuition telling you to do right now? Trust it and act.

Once in a while, I break free
from my appointment book.
I live at my own pace.

58

INSTINCT

Constantly living by appointments and deadlines created by your mind can make you crazy, wondering when joy left your life.

Leave your watch behind and trust your instincts and intuition to let you know when it's time to eat, sleep, work, and play. Be present to what is going on around you and respond naturally.

Evenings, weekends, and holidays are a great time to find your groove and flow. You might enjoy this so much that you try to find ways to live like this always.

I am inspired by others.
Their brilliance awakens
my brilliance.

 59

INSPIRATION

Your mindfulness practice will begin to reveal to you how we are all more alike than we are different. No one will do life quite the way you do but, deep inside, the human longings are the same in us all. We can learn from and elevate each other.

Find quotes and stories told by others that really resonate with you. What is it that touches you and calls to you? Allow those words to arouse your genius.

I defy labels.
I am an original.

60

ORIGINALITY

Labels are for clothes, not for people. When you identify yourself by the work you do or the roles you have, what you can and cannot do, or even what you like and dislike, you try to place limits on a limitless being. When you try to copy someone else, you become a cheap knock-off.

Give yourself the freedom to just BE and discover your own original style.

I give myself everything I need.
Others benefit
because I have more to give.

 61

SELFISHNESS

You came here to love and care for others and help them along their path, but never at your own expense.   Life never requires self-sacrifice.   You can't feed anyone else if you are starving.   Build your own stores of health, vitality, joy, and peace.   When you feel called to give, you can do so from a full heart.   Be a bit selfish so you can be more selfless.

I feel the music in me
and I move and flow.

62

MUSIC

Many traditions use music and movement as a form of meditation and a means to connect with Divinity. Play pieces that are soulful and have a strong beat. Clear a safe space and turn out the lights if you choose. Let the music move your body. BE in your body. Feel what it's like to move and flow with Life.

To everything there is a season.
I am in tune with the
natural timing of all things.

✿ 63

CYCLES

If you feel you are struggling, perhaps you are going against the natural cycles and flow of life. Pushing too hard or holding on too tight can block you from the good that is waiting for you.

Think of something that has become difficult for you. Ask what is needed at this time for your highest good to come. Riding the wave as it rises and falls in the NOW paradoxically allows you to always be on top.

Birds of a feather flock together.
I choose to be my best
so I receive the best.

64

MAGNETISM

Like attracts like. Notice the kind of people you attract, the circumstances that keep occurring in your life, the kind of thoughts you keep having. If there is something or someone you would rather not be associated with, look within for the magnetizing belief that you can amplify or release so you can soar with the eagles instead of scratching with the chickens.

When things seem
too heavy to bear,
I seek Divine assistance.

🪷 65

ASSISTANCE

At times it can feel like you alone are carrying the weight of the world on your shoulders. This will sap the energy that you need to live effectively and joyfully.

You don't have to do it all by yourself. In your mind, write a message asking for help onto a helium-filled balloon. Breathe deeply and slowly as you watch it float out of sight. Trust that a Higher Source receives your request. Be mindful of what shows up and act accordingly. Be grateful for the books, resources, and people that are sent your way.

Each day is a new day.
I make bold choices.

66

BEGINNINGS

As best you can, let go of any hurts or disappointments from yesterday. Remember, your power is in the present moment. Every day and every minute is an opportunity to start over, choose something new, more fulfilling, and more in line with who you are. Your life can change in an instant if you are brave enough to let it.

Go ahead, begin again.

It's okay if it's sometimes
hard to stay mindful.
I come back whenever I can.

🪷 67

PROGRESS

Be gentle with yourself. Mindfulness is not another "should." As you begin to let go of perfectionism, you can let go of trying to be perfectly mindful. This is a life-long journey. When you notice that you have strayed, just step back on the path. As with anything in life, progress is more important than perfection.

To get better answers,
I ask better questions.
I am a problem solver.

68

SOLUTIONS

You may be challenged at times by too many objections when you set an affirmation or intention. Flip it around and ask it as a question. "Why am I so richly abundant and financially free?" The mind loves to solve problems. It will get busy coming up with all kinds of answers and examples of why it's already true and more ways it can be true. Use your mind the way it was intended.

I immerse myself in
pastimes that bring me joy.
I live passionately.

🪷 69

PASSION

Have you ever gotten so wrapped up in a favorite activity that time either flew or stood still? That's mindfulness. Total immersion keeps your mind's idle and negative chatter at bay, fills your heart, and energizes your whole being. Making time for your passions is crucial work for a juicy and happy life.

I am deeply faithful to
myself and life.
I always find my way.

70

FAITH

You must let go of hope. Hope is an obstacle to peace because it is a sign of feeling doubt and powerlessness in the moment. Instead, stress will melt when you cultivate faith. Even when the outcome is uncertain, faith is the knowledge that you can deal with every situation as you live your purpose. There is always a way through, whether you manage it on your own, with the help of others, or with divine assistance.

Be still and feel your way into the truth of your strength. Have faith and know you will find your way.

I never, never, never give up.
My passion fuels my action.
I am determined.

 71

DETERMINATION

When you get quiet enough to hear what your heart truly wants, don't deny it. If people tell you it's impossible or unrealistic, smile because you know the depth of your determination. Connect with your passion and breathe deeply until that juice runs through you like a current of electricity. That power will carry you through challenging times and help you stay the course, resolving any blocks with grace, creativity, and joy.

I find time to be frivolous.
My heart is light and playful.

72

FRIVOLITY

All work and no play makes your life very boring. Sometimes the only thing that matters is fun. When it feels like things are becoming a chore, take five minutes for a guilty pleasure. Then drop the guilt and keep the pleasure. Guilt is a very destructive emotion. Pleasure makes life worthwhile.

Take a break to eat a chocolate bar, watch a funny video on YouTube®, kick a soccer ball, call a friend, or do a sudoku. You will be invigorated if you are mindful not to overindulge.

I wish I may, I wish I might, have the wish I wish tonight.

🪷 73

WISHING

Wishing is simpler and can be far more honest than setting goals and declaring intentions. Those can be ego-driven if you are not careful. You might tend to think that you are being silly or flippant when you wish. Actually, those are most likely the moments when your truest desires let themselves be known.

Step out into a starry, starry night. What do you wish for?

I use the tools in my
"inner peace toolbox"
to change my emotional state.

74 ❀

TOOLS

Choose words associated with peace such as *tranquility*, *serenity*, *harmony*, and *stillness*. Say these words silently and breathe their quality into your being.

Find poems, short stories, or sacred writings that comfort you and bring you peace.

Select music, pictures, and aromatherapy oils that resonate calmness in your body.

You might find an activity like yoga or walking in nature does the trick.

Get these tools ready for when you need them.

Sometimes the best way in is through the back door.

 75

BYPASS

If you find that your babbling Monkey Mind is particularly unruly and hard to control, you might have to bring out a tranquilizer gun.

Self-hypnosis CDs or subliminal recordings* can be a really effective tool to help you bypass your negative programming. By using these really simple methods, you can download new programming into your subconscious that will crowd out the old.

* You can get both a self-hypnosis and subliminal CD related to this book at my website. ☺

Visit www.LivingTheMindfulWay.com.

I can let go of any idea,
even if it is a good one.
I choose the ones to act on.

76

IDEAS

As you persist with opening your awareness, you will master the ability to let go of what does not serve you or your purpose.

As you open space, more positive thoughts and creative ideas will arrive. Don't let this trick you into taking on too much or going down the wrong path. Ideas are floating all around you. Some were meant for you to do, others were meant for you to pass to someone else, still others were just meant to be noticed. Where will you invest your energy?

My relationships reflect
Who I Am.
I interact lovingly with Life.

 77

RELATIONSHIP

You are connected to every person, place, thing, and circumstance in your life. Your entire life is an interaction. How you respond to whatever appears to be outside yourself is a reflection of the relationship between your mind and your heart. Every problem is a relationship problem and every success is a relationship success.

As you go through your day, or during your meditation time, notice the quality of your relationships. How do you interact with loved ones, co-workers, strangers, money, nature, politics, traffic, food, your home, body, time, and every other element of your experience? What do your relationships reveal?

What other people think of me
is none of my business.
I approve of myself.

78

SELF-RESPECT

You are the only one who can live your life. The more mindful you are and the better you get to know yourself, the less it will matter to you what other people think. The deeper your connection with your Self, the less you will feel the need to fit in and seek the approval of others. Respect yourself and trust your own wisdom.

May all beings be well
and happy.
May there be peace.

🪷 79

KINDNESS

Extending loving kindness to yourself and to all beings is one of the fastest ways to find peace. Look around you and notice where there is a deficit of love. Open your heart and send blessings of good will to yourself, your family and friends, your community, the world, all living creatures, and Mother Earth. In those moments, there will be no room for thoughts leading to pain or suffering. In those moments, you will know only peace.

I love and forgive my family.
My heart is big enough
to release the past and be happy.

80

FAMILY

Read Tips 14 and 41 again. Through this filter, extend compassion to your parents and other family members. No matter how loving they were or how messed up they were, the odds were stacked against them. It was inevitable that your innocent child self would have some emotional hurts and scars.

It's time to end the feud. Love and forgive your family and yourself. You all do the best you can.

I do only what is mine to do.
I let others do what is theirs to do.

❀ 81

UNLOADING

It is easy to take on responsibilities that belong to those you care about. But the weight of it diverts energy from your own life, becoming a burden because it isn't yours. Review Tip 41.

Imagine you are at the beach with someone whose load you are shouldering. Write it on a beach ball with a big marker. Then, with love, gently toss that beach ball to the rightful owner. Feel your relief and peace as the weight lifts from you. Give yourself permission to follow through.

It's all good news.
Even bad news
is a blessing when I'm mindful.

82

MASTERY

As your understanding of who you are expands, you might choose to try a more advanced practice. If you desire self mastery, the state of mind*less*ness and joy, true freedom and peace, you can consciously delve deeper.

Turn on the evening (not the late) news. Be aware of all your reactions to the events on the screen. What is being revealed about your subconscious programming? What passes by without comment and what hooks you? Is there something you would like to explore and master now that you have the capacity?

I am happy to be alive.
Life is a blessing.

 83

BLESSINGS

When you slow down to notice the beauty all around you, you will see what a miracle creation is. What a blessing, what joy.

Oh, did you notice that you are part of it all? What a blessing you are, what a joy you are.

I end my day on a high.
I count my blessings
and sleep peacefully.

84 ✿

SLEEP

Just as your state at the start of your day sets the tone for your waking hours, your state at the end of the day sets the tone for your resting hours.

Acknowledge when you were present throughout the day and aware of what was going on around you. Think about constructive choices you made and thank yourself. Be grateful for the gifts. These are good thoughts to fall asleep to. What you think about expands. Sweet dreams!

I AM.

🪷 85

ONENESS

Breathe. Expand. Become one with all that is.

Welcome home!

SPECIAL REPORT

THE COURAGE TO ASK

How One Simple Question Will Empower You
To Open Your Heart, Heal Old Wounds,
Be Gentle, Patient, and Light-Hearted,
Free Yourself and Others of Limitations,
Look Beyond the Surface for Deep Meaning,
Live In a State of Child-Like Wonder,
Become the Master of Your Destiny, and
Totally Rock Your World

To get your FREE copy
and other resources,
Visit www.LivingTheMindfulWay.com

To order more copies of this book,
Visit www.LivingTheMindfulWayBook.com